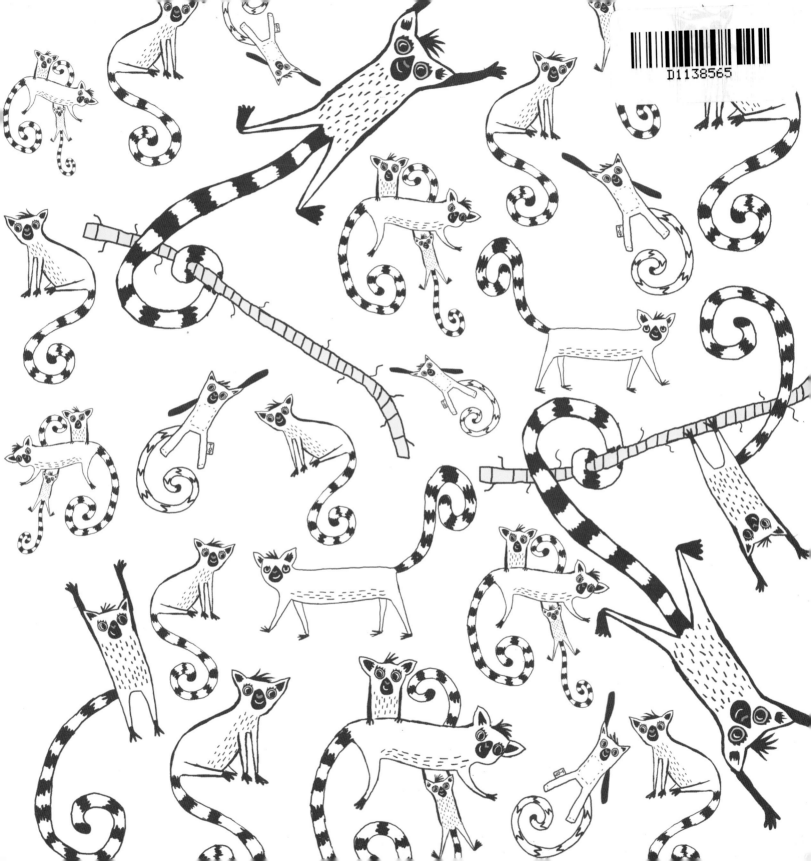

Opticians

Boots Opticians
D90, Thane Road,
Beeston, Nottingham, NG90 1BS
boots.com/opticians

Published by Boots Opticians

Text © copyright Boots Opticians
Illustrations © copyright Boots Opticians
Typesetting, layout, editing and design © copyright Boots Opticians

A catalogue record for this book is available from the British Library

ISBN 978-0-9935589-0-0

Printed in the United Kingdom

FSC
www.fsc.org
MIX
From responsible
sources
FSC® C003009

ZOOKEEPER ZOE

FOREWORD

As a parent I know there are one million things to think about, but making sure your child can see properly is so important. My daughter Princess wears glasses and so I know how essential it is to ensure your kids get the proper eye health checks they need.

That's why I'm supporting this fun storybook from Boots Opticians with four vision checks built into the story. We hope to remind parents that all children should have a regular eye health check at least every two years from around the age of three.

Pass it on! Around 80% of what a child learns is through sight, yet there are an estimated one million children in the UK with an undiagnosed vision problem. Together, by sharing this book, we can make a huge difference. Once you have enjoyed Zookeeper Zoe's adventure with your children, please pass it on to other families to help every child reach their full potential.

Happy reading!
Peter Andre

USING THIS BOOK

At Boots Opticians we know that good vision is vital in helping children reach their full potential. Zookeeper Zoe allows parents and carers to check a child's visual capability whilst reading for pleasure.

While you enjoy reading this book with your child, keep a note of their responses to the questions that appear next to the ⦿ eye symbol. There is guidance at the back of the book to assist you in identifying whether your child may need help with their vision or if they have difficulty identifying particular colours.

1

Ensure your room is well lit before you start.

2

If your child already wears glasses or contact lenses, make sure they are wearing them.

3

If prompted, ask your child to cover one eye to complete the check.

4

Follow the guidance provided for each check.

LET'S GET STARTED

If there ever was a child who loved animals, it was Zoe.

She read about rhinos,

she watched films about flamingos,

she was crazy about crocs and barmy for bears.

She laughed at lemurs and smiled at snakes,
but elephants were her favourite of all.

HA
HA
HA

WHAT'S
YOUR
FAVOURITE
ANIMAL?

There wasn't a single creature that she didn't like.
When she grew up, Zoe wanted to be a zookeeper.

Every weekend Zoe begged her parents to take her to the zoo.

After all, how was she going to become a zookeeper if she never met the animals?

When they finally agreed, Zoe could barely hide her excitement.
She packed a big bag with everything she thought she'd need.

But when Zoe and her parents arrived at the zoo, the gates were shut! The zookeeper looked upset. He didn't want to close the zoo, but there was far too much work for one person.

CHECK 1

- Hold the book at arm's length and ask your child to fully cover one eye
- Ask your child whether any of the black lines at the top of the zoo gates look darker and clearer than the others?
- Now ask them to fully cover their other eye and check again

"I can help you!" said Zoe. "I know lots about animals. Maybe I could be your assistant?"

"Yes, please," said the zookeeper.
"There are so many jobs to do! Shall we start with the bear?"

"Boris says he's hungry," explained the zookeeper,
"but he won't even look at his salmon sandwich."

"Salmon?" said Zoe. "No wonder!"

And she pulled from her bag a big, soft and totally delicious
peanut butter and cucumber sandwich.

"That should do the trick," said Zoe. And it did!
The zookeeper looked impressed.

"What next?" asked Zoe.

WHICH SANDWICH WOULD YOU CHOOSE? SALMON, OR PEANUT BUTTER AND CUCUMBER?

When they got to the elephant, it was clear that she wasn't happy.
"It's Ellie's birthday today," muttered the zookeeper. "And, well, I… forgot."

"Not to worry," said Zoe. "I've got just the thing."

From her bag she pulled out a fabulous, fancy birthday cake.
There were also some beautiful birthday balloons, sure to make Ellie smile.

CHECK 2

- Hold the book at arm's length
- Ask your child to look at all of Ellie's birthday balloons
- Can they identify or trace the number on each balloon with their finger?

"Happy birthday, Ellie!"
Zoe said. The zookeeper –
and the elephant – looked
impressed.

"What next?"
asked Zoe.

Zoe knew as soon as she saw the cheeky lemurs causing chaos that all they needed was a good story to calm them down…

... and that the flamingos just wanted something to dance to.

- Hold the book at arm's length and ask your child to fully cover one eye
- Ask your child to look at the circles on Zoe's stereo
- Ask your child if the circles look darker and clearer on either the red or green background
- Ask them to cover the other eye fully and check again

It turned out that the tiger
needed a tennis partner…

… and the gorilla just wanted everyone to give him back the cards they'd hidden so that he could play his favourite game in peace…

CHECK 4

- Hold the book three metres away from your child
- Ask your child to fully cover one eye
- Point to the symbols on the blanket in front of the gorilla
- Ask your child to tell you which animal is holding the matching cards

CHECK 4

- Continue to hold the book three metres away from your child
- Ask your child to fully cover the other eye
- Point to the symbols on the blanket in front of the gorilla
- Ask your child to tell you which animal is holding the matching cards

... which they did! And when the tiger was tired of tennis, he joined in too!

Zoe was rather pleased with her morning's work, and so was the zookeeper. He could open the zoo to visitors once again.

"I don't know how you did it," the zookeeper said to Zoe,
"but that was amazing. You're a natural!"

"When can I start?" Zoe asked, excitedly.
"I think you already have!" the zookeeper laughed.

THE END

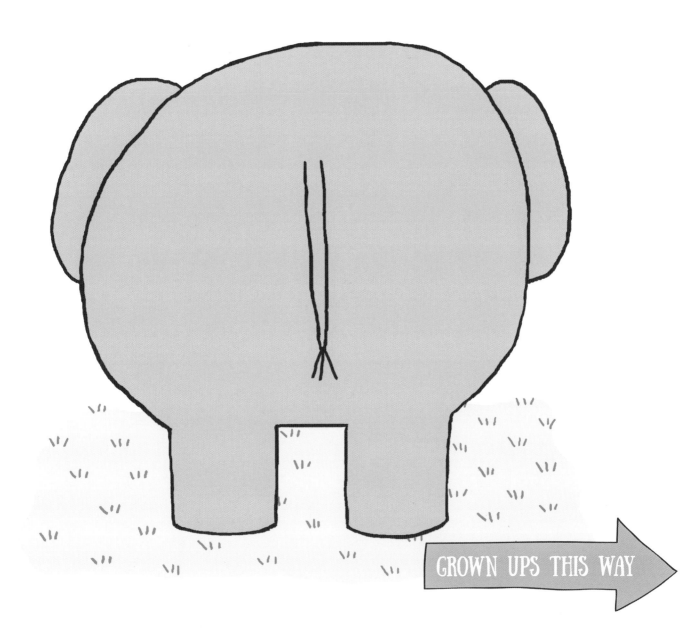

GROWN UPS THIS WAY →

UNDERSTANDING THE RESULTS

You might want to consider booking your child in for a full eye health check with a trained optometrist if the answer is **YES** to any of the following questions:

◉ CHECK 1: Astigmatism check

Did your child think that some of the lines in this image were darker and clearer than others?

Asitgmatism is when the curve of the front surfaces of the eye effects focusing. This check helps to identify astigmatism.

◉ CHECK 2: Colour vision check

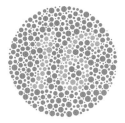

Was your child unable to trace or identify any of the numbers in the balloons correctly?

This helps to identify how well different colours are distinguished.

◉ CHECK 3: Duochrome check

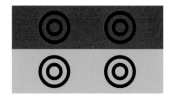

Did your child think some of the circles on the stereo appeared darker and clearer than the others?

This helps to check the ability of the eyes to focus correctly.

◉ CHECK 4: Visual acuity check

Did your child struggle to tell you which animal was holding the matching card?

Visual acuity is the accuracy and sharpness of your vision in distinguishing detail.

TO BOOK AN EYE HEALTH CHECK APPOINTMENT

A full eye health check at your local Boots Opticians will check your child's sight and the health of their eyes. That's why we recommend a regular eye check at least every two years from the age of three.

Eye checks are **FREE** for children under 16, funded by the NHS.

Three easy ways to book an eye check at Boots Opticians:

 Call **0345 125 3752**

 Visit **www.boots.com/opticians**

 Find your local practice **www.boots.com/storelocator**

Pass it on

We'd love you to help us find the estimated one million children in the UK who can't see properly. Please give this book to a family you know to help their child reach their full potential.

   Share your story: #ZookeeperZoe

Together, we can help every family learn about the importance of eye health. Please use **#ZookeeperZoe** to share your stories about eye health and the pleasure of reading.

"#ZookeeperZoe is great! The story is such fun and being able to check my kid's eyes at the same time made it even better. Thank you, Boots!" Alice, Tunbridge Wells

 ## National Literacy Trust

The National Literacy Trust is a charity dedicated to raising literacy levels in the UK. We work to improve the reading, writing, speaking and listening skills in the UK's most disadvantaged communities, campaign to make literacy a priority for politicians, parents and support schools. Find out more at **www.literacytrust.org.uk**

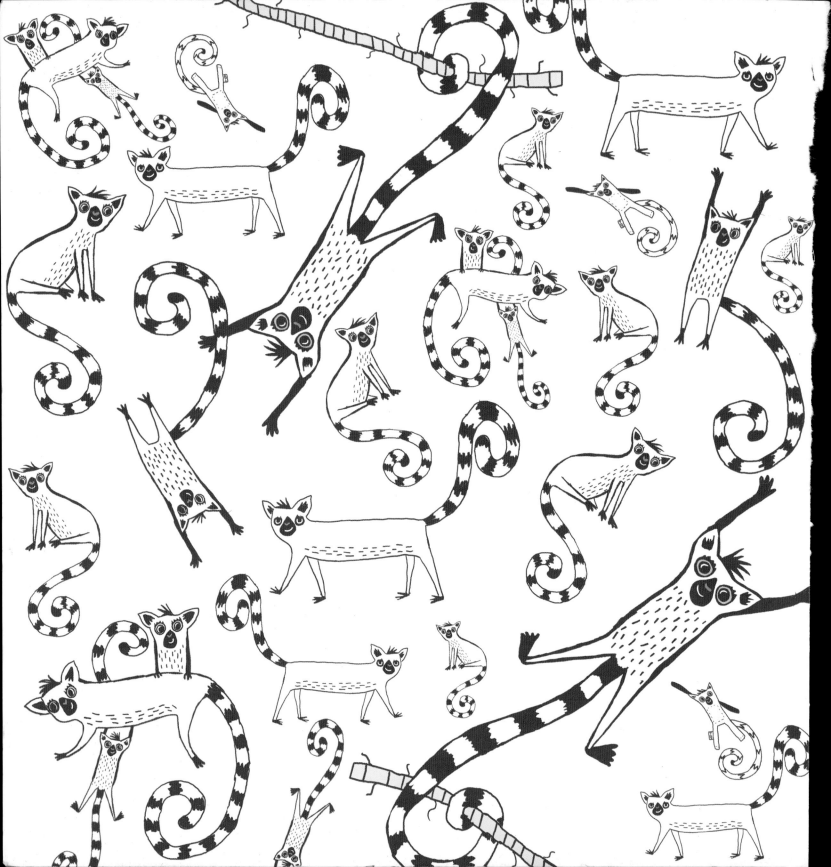